Adoption

Questions and Feelings About ...

W
FRANKLIN WATTS
LONDON • SYDNEY

Anita Ganeri
Illustrated by Ximena Jeria

Franklin Watts
First published in Great Britain in 2018 by The Watts Publishing Group

Editor: Melanie Palmer
Design: Lisa Peacock
Author: Anita Ganeri
Consultant: Jo Mitchell

ISBN: 978 1 4451 6444 1 (Hbk)
ISBN: 978 1 4451 6445 8 (Pbk)

Printed in China

FSC
www.fsc.org
MIX
Paper from
responsible sources
FSC® C104740

Franklin Watts
An imprint of
Hachette Children's Group
Part of The Watts Publishing Group
Carmelite House
50 Victoria Embankment
London EC4Y 0DZ

An Hachette UK Company
www.hachette.co.uk

www.franklinwatts.co.uk

Adoption

Being part of a family is special. You care for each other. You have fun together. You fall out with each other. You make up.

Your parents look after you as you grow up.
They help to keep you safe.

*How does it feel
to be part of
your family?*

There are many ways of making a family. Some families have a mum and a dad. Some have two mums, or two dads. Some have just one parent.

Sometimes, parents can't live together and they split up. They might find other partners. Then you might have a step-mum or a step-dad.

Who is in your family?

The family you're born into is called your birth family. Sometimes, children cannot live with their birth families.

This might be because their birth parents are ill or finding it hard to look after themselves. They cannot look after the children or keep them safe.

If children can't live with their birth families, they may be adopted. This means that they go to live with a new family.

Some children are adopted when they're babies. Some are adopted when they're older. Some children are adopted with their brothers or sisters.

Social workers are people who look for a new family. They visit the family at home and meet the mum and dad. They also meet any family pets.

They come back for lots more visits. They ask the family lots of questions to make sure that it will be the right family for the child.

Some children live with a foster family until they can go to their new family. They may stay for a few months or, sometimes, a few years.

The foster family may have other children staying with them. They may have their own children living with them, too.

The big day comes when the child meets his or her new family. This might be just for a few hours or a day at first. This helps everyone to get to know each other.

Meeting a new family can be exciting but scary.
The child, and the new mum and dad, might feel
very shy.

If everything goes well, the child moves into the new family's house. He or she may have a new bedroom to put their things in. This helps the child to feel at home.

What makes you feel at home?

Later, when the child has settled in, it is time to meet other members of the family.

Starting at a new school can feel scary.
It can feel hard to try to make new friends.

How did you feel when you started school?

School friends may wonder what being adopted means. They may ask questions that the child isn't able to answer.

Being adopted can feel confusing. It can be hard for children to understand why they can't live with their birth parents.

Children who are adopted as babies may not remember their birth parents. If they are older, they may not have happy memories.

What makes you feel confused?

Children might wonder why their new family wanted to adopt them.

Their new mum might say that she couldn't grow a baby in her tummy. She wanted to adopt a child because she wanted to have a family.

When children are adopted, they are given a book with their life story in it. There might be photos of their birth family in the book.

The children can look through the book with their forever family. It can help them to understand why they were adopted.

It's important to know who you are, and where you came from. It's important to feel proud of who you are.

What would you say or do to cheer someone up?

Being adopted means being part of a family that love you and keep you safe. That's something to feel proud of, too.

Notes for parents and teachers

This book can be a useful way for families and professionals to begin a discussion with children about what it means to be adopted. Adopted children may feel shy or vulnerable in a group situation so it is important to be as inclusive as possible. Choice of appropriate vocabulary when discussing adoption is important. For example, rather than using a term like 'real parents' use 'first parents', 'biological parents' or 'birth parents' and avoid any generalisations.

Sometimes children may be given projects at school that involve details of their family life, such as creating family trees, discussing family pictures, bringing in baby pictures, or making timelines. For an adopted child, many of these may cause them to feel left out and uncomfortable, so it is good to have a strategy for broader activities such as those mentioned on page 31.

Adoptive children may require extra support at any stage of their childhood so it is important they are able to identify someone they can trust and talk to safely – whether an adult, friend, or an organisation, that can provide support and understanding. Teaching about empathy and the diveristy of family life and the varied make ups of a family will help equip children to understand there are many similarities, as well as differences, between them all.

Classroom or group activities

1. Ask the children to create a 'Who's in My World?' drawing which can include any significant people who are not necessarily direct relations. It might include family friends, teachers, community members, babysitters, pets and so on. You could discuss how families are often made up of many people who aren't always just blood relations.

2. Conduct a survey by asking the children to pinpoint one significant moment in their life development - whether it is riding a bike for the first time, learning to swim, discovering a new place or tasting something amazing or anything else that they feel was significant to them. It could be something from school or a school trip. You could create a picture chart of all the answers to show the variety of what informs their lives, ensuring no one is excluded.

3. Reading a story such as one from a picture book that features adoption as a theme can be a good way to introduce the topic to a class. It could also be used as a starting point to then ask children to create their own story about someone being adopted, which would encourage and develop empathy.

Further Information

Books

My Parents Picked Me: A First Look at Adoption by Pat Thomas and Lesley Harker (Wayland, 2003)

Tyler's Wishes: A book for children being adopted by Helen Kahn and Sarah Rawlings (British Association for Adoption and Fostering, 2003)

Who's in My Family? by Robie H. Harris and Nadine Bernard Westcott (Walker, 2015)

Websites

adoptionuk.org – Charity supporting parents and children in the adoption process

familylives.org.uk – Provides advice on a range of issues including adoption and fostering

pac-uk.org – An agency providing essential adoption support and advice